TORONTO

The Heart of the City

TORONTO
The Heart of the City

Foreword by Mayor Arthur C. Eggleton

KEY PORTER BOOKS

**Canadian Cataloguing
in Publication Data**

Main entry under title:

Toronto, the heart of the city

ISBN 1-55013-083-8

1. Toronto (Ont.) — Description —
Views.

FC3097.37.T67 1988   971.3′54104′0222
C88-093022-5
F1059.5.T6843T67 1988

Key Porter Books Limited
70 The Esplanade
Toronto, Ontario
Canada M5E 1R2

Design: First Image
Typesetting: First Image
Printed and bound in Belgium

88 89 90 91   6 5 4 3 2 1

Photograph page 2: Streetcars have carried
commuters to and from work in Toronto
for more than a hundred years.

Contents

Foreword

This impressive review of the city of Toronto has been published within a dozen years of the millennium and the end of a century in which this country, Canada, has taken its place on the world stage. Toronto has emerged as Canada's gateway to the world and the city where so many people see Canada for the first time.

What they see, and what I believe in, is a city of balances: a city where old and new Canadians live in harmony; where people from every corner of the globe have come to make their home; where neighbourhoods thrive and people cherish their heritage and their roots; where no culture need feel threatened and where everyone is welcome; where citizens have created a quality of life that is recognized around the world.

Our ancestors left with us not only a spirit of community, but a strong sense of civility in the way we do things. That enormous fact has meant more to this city than is yet realized.

Cities are recognized in many ways: for their architecture, for example — the brilliance of the new and the restoration and preservation of the old — and for the respect people have for each other and their surroundings. Cities are also admired for their vitality, and in this respect, as well as in more traditional terms, Toronto offers an extraordinary diversity of culture and heritage — a diversity that is almost by itself one of the key reasons why Toronto is now unique.

I commend the reader to these pages, to what they present and to what they represent. To know this city is not difficult because knowing our people is easy, and that is especially so if you become the camera and experience Toronto personally.

As Mayor of Toronto, I am delighted to offer this message and trust that you will not only enjoy this book, but its subject as well, in the years to come.

Sincerely,

Arthur C. Eggleton
Mayor
The City of Toronto

Opposite page: Kensington Market may be the most culturally diverse of the city's markets.

The Comfortable City

"Toronto will be a fine town when it's finished."

Brendan Behan

Toronto was begun by Upper Canada's first lieutenant-governor, John Graves Simcoe, who ordered the first city plan to be drawn up in 1793. A man of energy, enthusiasm and vision, Simcoe discovered a region of dense bush on the shores of Lake Ontario and saw there a fine harbour, a defensible military base, a ship-building site and the potential centre of continental trade. The settlement that was subsequently established was called York. It grew slowly, at first. Its importance in its early years was not so much a reflection of its founder's vision as the result of the concentration of garrison and government within its boundaries

By the time of its incorporation in 1834, Toronto, with a population of nine thousand, was beginning to show some of the promise that Simcoe had foreseen. Besides government buildings, there was a market, church, school, more than a hundred and fifty houses (some, like The Grange, quite imposing) and several taverns. One of the taverns, Montgomery's, figured in the rebellion of 1837, but by and large, Toronto's growth in succeeding decades was steady and peaceful.

Toronto became the nexus of transportation beginning with the development of railroads in the 1850s. Later it became a financial and banking centre, rivalling and finally overtaking, Montreal in importance. It became one of the major industrial cities in Canada, producing everything from processed food to heavy machinery. And culturally, Toronto may be compared to other great cities in that its artists now define their own trends and fashions, and do not slavishly follow those invented elsewhere.

Who knows what Toronto may yet become? The city as the Irish playwright, Brendan Behan, observed, is incomplete. Toronto is still actively engaged in the process of making itself.

Visitors will find that the progress made so far is impressive. Toronto's plain grid of streets forms the basis of what may be the most efficient public transit system in North America. Its neighbourhoods, from Cabbagetown to Rosedale, are comfortable, attractive and well-maintained. And throughout the city there are parks, green and pleasant sanctuaries, that make the most of Toronto's topographical assets, the modest rivers and wide lake.

The most striking features of Toronto, perhaps, are not the sky-high buildings, the underground plazas, or any other aspect of what might be called the city's "physical plant," but the perception shared by almost every visitor and resident that all this modern urban technology is in the service of the citizen, and not the other way round.

Toronto is unfinished, but other cities may well envy the start it has made.

Opposite page: A Chinatown vendor shows off the pick of his produce.

The current spate of high-rise development is creating a towering wall of concrete and glass along the waterfront.

Opposite page: Cabbagetown, one of the city's older residential neighbourhoods, assumes a comfortable, tumbledown aspect in winter.

Signs inside the streetcars wisely advise
passengers to "Keep Arm In," but in
summer the temptation to disobedience can
be irresistible.

The network of streetcars, buses and subways makes up one of the most efficient urban transport systems in North America.

The double-decker passenger cars of GO
Transit bring commuters into Toronto from
as far away as Hamilton.

Opposite page: Lester B. Pearson International
Airport takes its name from one of Canada's
most internationally-minded prime
ministers.

Shoppers can make their way from the
subway at Yorkdale to one of the city's
largest shopping centres by way of a covered
passage.

The Don Valley Parkway is one of the three principal expressways connecting downtown to the outlying boroughs.

Following pages: Toronto by night.

Toronto's founder, John Graves Simcoe,
reckoned the harbour was the finest on
Lake Ontario.

In winter the lakefront, because it's so exposed to the elements, can be bitterly cold.

Many of the homes on Toronto Island are eccentric as well as attractive.

Opposite page: Rampant gentrification in Parkdale has made parts of a plain neighbourhood pretty.

Avenue Road at Chaplin Crescent: an established residential neighbourhood.

Above: A mural on Queen Street West creates a surreal effect.

Right: Blocks are frequently bisected by alleys in Toronto's older sections. They offer visitors an intimate view of the city's architecture.

A renovated Victorian townhouse in
Cabbagetown.

A corner store in Cabbagetown makes fun of the neighbourhood's name.

Following pages: The park which borders on Cabbagetown is informal, but the botanical display inside the Allan Gardens greenhouse is magnificent.

Dundas Street near Spadina Avenue is the
focus of one of the largest Chinese
communities in North America.

The stalls are almost always busy in the
streets of Chinatown.

Another aspect of Toronto's ethnic diversity:
a thriving Polish community has been
established east of High Park.

Opposite page: High Park, given to the city in
1873 by an architect, John Howard, is a
large and leafy refuge from urban turmoil.

The Harris Filtration Plant, at the eastern
end of the Beaches, offers a terraced
prospect over Lake Ontario.

Above: The Scarborough Bluffs rise three hundred feet above the lake.

Right: The city's core is dotted with miniature parks like this one at the intersection of Dundas and Bay.

Real and artificial waterfowl mingle in the
park on Centre Island.

Gull-chasing on the lakefront.

The Sights to See

"It must be fun!"

Raymond Moriyama

Acommunity may know itself by its buildings. Architects, and the city elders who commission them, may mould their own and their citizens' sense of identity by the public buildings they erect. This insight may lead the visitor to some surprising conclusions about Torontonians.

The city's older buildings reveal what might be expected, given the overwhelming English and Celtic influence on its early development. The Victorian eclecticism of the Annex, and the vaguely Gothic aspect of St. James Cathedral, are perhaps typical of the city's first hundred-or-so years. They are staid at best, rather homely at worst. And whether homely or staid, they hark back to a distant original.

Of course, there are exceptions. St. Lawrence Hall, lovingly restored in the 1960s, has about it an air of cheerful self-confidence. Old City Hall, built of local and New Brunswick sandstone, exudes a glow that is both welcoming and dignified. Casa Loma is one of a kind: a glorious folly precisely reflecting the eccentricity of its first owner.

Such structures serve to prove the rule. Most of what Toronto has inherited from its early years is derivative and uninspired. But look what is happening now! Bank towers made of gold! A mall designed to resemble an ocean liner! A library built around a five-storey atrium like an empty teacup! A domed stadium that can be opened to the sky!

The high-rise towers that now dominate Toronto's skyline are condemned by some as vulgar, admired by others as massive sculptures, or monuments to the unfettered human spirit. They are undeniably brash. They appear to be so far removed from the quiet reserve so often equated with the spirit that animates Toronto as to have no connection at all.

The New City Hall, which was opened in 1965, appears now to have been a watershed. Some of the finest public buildings constructed since then share its virtues: they are bold, imaginative, useful and fun. The Ontario Science Centre, designed by architect Raymond Moriyama, typifies the style. It is made up of three linked pavilions, inspired by the three-petalled provincial flower, the trillium. The connecting corridors flow down the steep sides of a ravine. It, too, is both serviceable and exciting.

The new Toronto, to judge by its buildings, is also fun.

Opposite page: The New City Hall — actually Toronto's fourth — was opened in 1965.

Casa Loma, a Toronto landmark, was the creation of an eccentric capitalist, Sir Henry Pellatt.

Opposite page: Old City Hall, across the street from the new, was built at the turn of the century.

The Metro Convention Centre attracts
trade shows, conferences and seminars from
all over the continent.

The Toronto Stock Exchange moved into its new quarters at King and York streets in 1983.

Sculpture and mural at either end of the park on Front Street.

Opposite page: The Gooderham Building, built in 1892, housed the offices of banker and businessman, George Gooderham.

The flight of geese was created on
commission for the Eaton Centre by artist
Michael Snow.

The Scarborough Civic Centre includes municipal offices, a shopping mall, and a pond that doubles as a skating rink.

Roy Thomson Hall, designed by Arthur Erickson, is the home of the Toronto Symphony Orchestra.

Opposite page: The Ontario Legislative Building has been the seat of government in the province since 1893.

The Robarts Library, "Fort Book" to many of its users, is the University of Toronto's principal research and graduate library.

Opposite page: The University of Toronto is Canada's largest and, arguably, its most prestigious university.

Right: Although the original buildings are long gone, Upper Canada College has been a Toronto institution since the 1830s.

Right: The cow, by sculptor Joseph Fafard, seems to be surprisingly comfortable on Wellington Street.

Opposite page: The city's banks have, in many cases, abandoned imposing buildings such as this one on Yonge Street, for more modern structures.

Allan Gardens maintains a varied and
beautiful display of plants all year inside the
greenhouse, and when weather permits, in
the surrounding park.

Opposite page: Despite appearances the CN
Tower, on the left, is hundreds of feet taller
than the light standard on the right.

George Brown, the founder and editor of
The Globe newspaper, lived in this imposing
house until his death from a gunshot
wound in 1880.

One admiring observer called the new Royal Bank Plaza "architecture as abstract sculpture." It was opened in 1976.

Victoria College, University of Toronto, was
founded by Methodists, but now has no
religious affiliation.

St. James Cathedral is the fourth church on the site. The first opened its doors in 1807.

The wrought-iron gate outside Osgoode Hall was useful a century ago to keep cows out of the grounds.

Opposite page: St. Lawrence Hall, one of the most attractive older buildings in downtown Toronto, can be rented for public functions.

Osgoode Hall was opened in 1832 as the
home of the Law Society of Upper Canada.

Old City Hall reflected in the mirrored
glass of an adjacent building.

City Lights

"Nobody should visit Toronto for the first time."

Allan Lamport

An eminent visitor to Toronto in the early years of this century made a virtue of the fact that there was little to do. With Massey Hall the only stage in town, he explained, he attended the concerts, plays and recitals it offered as a matter of course. In London, by way of contrast, with so much to choose from, he rarely found the time to go out. Following this logic, the same visitor might be as idle today in Toronto as he was then in London. There is almost too much to do.

In Toronto in 1900, a visitor might have seen the best of British and American theatre in touring productions. If he were alive today, he could see Broadway smashes at the O'Keefe Centre and British hits creditably re-created at the Royal Alexandra Theatre. He could also see Canadian plays on any one of a dozen-or-so stages across the city. Canadian theatre might surprise him. The acting style and dialogue have a casual directness, distinct from the British manner, that is easily underrated. Taken on its own terms it is frequently powerful stuff.

After he had exhausted the theatrical possibilities (if they had not exhausted him first) a visitor in modern Toronto will find any number of other diversions. The Metro Zoo, situated on more than seven hundred acres in the eastern part of the city, is generally acknowledged to be one of the best in the world. The Royal Ontario Museum, with a mandate that embraces natural history and art, as well as archeology, is also one of the finest institutions in its sphere. The Art Gallery of Ontario, with its collection of contemporary Canadian work, and the huge bequest of Henry Moore, is unique.

On a less rarified plane, a visitor who arrives in late summer or early fall might enjoy attending the Canadian National Exhibition (the largest of its kind in the world) or the Royal Agricultural Winter Fair. And, for anyone for whom a big-league sporting event is culture enough, the Blue Jays baseball team, the Argonauts football team, and the Maple Leafs hockey team, all play to knowledgeable and enthusiastic (and in the case of the Maple Leafs, relentlessly optimistic) audiences.

Perhaps our visitor from an earlier time would have found it all too much. And perhaps this is what Allan Lamport, an ebullient Toronto mayor in the early 1950s, meant when he inveighed against those who visit the city for the first time. It may all be too much to assimilate in one go.

In which case, the only sensible advice is to visit not once, but again and again.

Opposite page: Fireworks over Ontario Place.

Ontario Place, described by one critic as
"five oil rigs off the lakeshore," is one of the
half-dozen most popular theme parks in the
world.

HMCS *Haida*, famous for her exploits in convoy duty during the Second World War, is permanently at anchor near Ontario Place.

Ontario Place, operated by the provincial
government, welcomes between three and
four million visitors a year.

Opposite page: In summer yachtsmen test
their skills on Lake Ontario.

Following pages: The Canadian National
Exhibition, or "The Ex," is the world's
largest annual exhibition.

The O'Keefe Centre is Toronto's principal venue for ballet, opera and Broadway musicals.

Above: The Henry Moore Sculpture Centre
at the Art Gallery of Ontario attracts visitors
(young and old) from all over the world.

Right: The permanent collection of the Art
Gallery of Ontario includes European
masterpieces and the work of contemporary
Canadian artists.

Theatre-goers gather outside the "Royal
Alex" on a summer evening.

Opposite page: Cawthra Mulock told the
architect he wanted "the finest theatre on
the continent." The Royal Alexandra
Theatre, completed in 1907, is plush and
impressive.

Maple Leaf Gardens, perhaps best-known as
the home of the Toronto Maple Leafs
hockey team, is also the site of rock concerts
and circuses.

The entertainment offered at Harbourfront
ranges from poetry readings to concerts.

The Ontario Science Centre attracts more
than a million visitors a year.

Opposite page: The Metro Zoo, situated on
over seven hundred acres at the eastern end
of the city, was designed as much for the
comfort of the animals as for the
convenience of visitors.

The curatorial staff of the Royal Ontario
Museum collects, studies, and displays items
pertaining to both natural history and
archeology, as well as works of art.

Black Creek Pioneer Village, "a living museum," recreates pioneer life in a quiet corner of the borough of Downsview.

Following pages: Old crafts, such as hand-weaving, are demonstrated by skilled practitioners in the pioneer village.

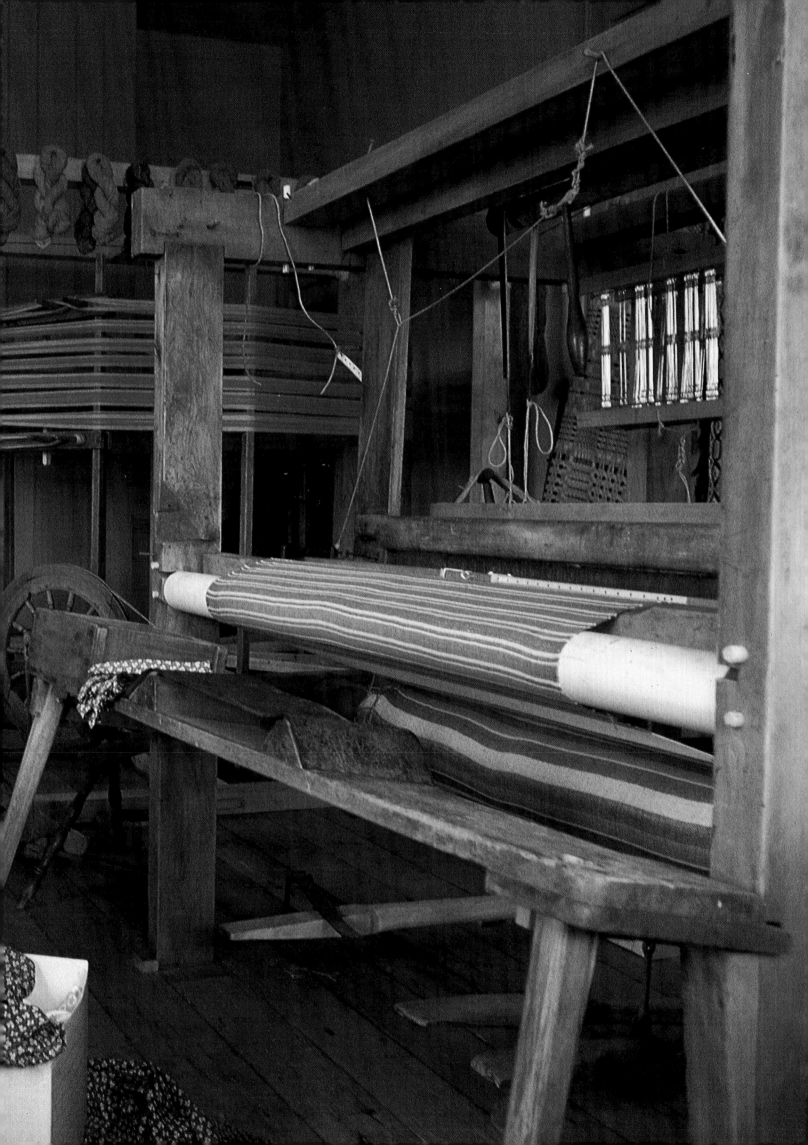

Film crews producing feature films and
episodes of television programmes seem to
be everywhere on the streets of "Hollywood
North."

The Festival of Festivals has become one of the most important film festivals in the world.

For twenty years, the city's West Indian community has participated in an annual celebration called "Caribana."

Opposite page: Perhaps the most spectacular element in Caribana is the parade.

A youthful athlete shows off his prowess on
a trampoline at Harbourfront.

An improvised ramp helps a skateboarder take off.

The Toronto Argonauts are perennial
contenders for the Grey Cup which denotes
dominance of the Canadian Football
League.

Fans watch the action at Exhibition Stadium.

Riverdale Farm gives urban kids a glimpse of rural life.

Opposite page: Youngsters in Forest Hill ski, slide and have snowball fights in winter, in Chatsworth Ravine.

Outfielder Jesse Barfield is one of several
members of the Toronto Blue Jays baseball
team who has thrilled fans in recent years.

An early-morning workout at Greenwood
Race Track.

Members of the West Toronto Lawn
Bowling Club demonstrate excellent form
on a summer afternoon.

Opposite page: The Don Valley Golf Course
is an unexpected island of peace near the
tumultuous Highway 401.

A Shopper's City

"Everything I like to do, I can do in Toronto."

Pauline McGibbon

ACanadian journalist in Moscow at the time of President Nixon's visit in 1972 is supposed to have asked the Soviet leader, Leonid Breshnev, how many Soviet missiles were pointed at Toronto. Breshnev, according to the story, answered: "None. I have nothing against the Italians."

The obvious point of the story, that Breshnev had confused "Toronto" with "Torino," is most likely the real point. It is just possible, however, that Breshnev knew better than his listeners of what he spoke. Toronto is the home of more than three hundred thousand people of Italian descent, making it one of the largest communities of its kind outside Italy.

Other ethnic groups make their presence seen and felt in the city. Toronto's Chinatown is one of the biggest in North America. There is a vibrant Portuguese community. Also a Greek, Hungarian, Latin and South American, East Indian, West Indian, Polish. . . . Successive waves of immigration have given Toronto a multicultural and polyglot texture, the exact make-up of which is unlike that of any other city in the world.

It can be seen most vividly in the markets. In Kensington Market, the exotic fruit and fresh fish are the stuff of Caribbean cooking. Around the corner there is a Mexican shop selling *tortillas*, peppers and dried beans. On St. Clair Avenue, baskets full of plum tomatoes are bought in season to be bottled and put up for another year's worth of simmering Italian sauces. On the Danforth, the bakeries sell Greek dainties, and on Broadview, on Sundays, the air has the spicy aroma of a Far Eastern kitchen. St. Lawrence Market has a bit of almost everything.

Of course, the shopper's want-list does not stop at foodstuffs. Toronto's retail precincts run the gamut, from Honest Ed's Bargain House on Bloor Street West, to the luxurious discretion of Hazelton Lanes. Somewhere between these extremes are the malls. The Eaton Centre employs some fifteen thousand people and encloses about three million square feet of floor space. On weekends Queen's Quay, in the attractive and diverting environment of Harbourfront, brings in the shoppers and browsers in droves.

Fred Gardiner, the first chairman of Metro Toronto and an undoubted booster, boasted of the city: "It is where big business is located, where big money, big decisions and big reputations are made. It . . . draws the restless, the energetic and the ambitious, the young men and women who want to be at the centre of things. . . ."

He was right. And like Pauline McGibbon, a former lieutenant-governor of the province of Ontario, those who are attracted to the city soon find that they have no need to go anywhere else.

Opposite page: Fresh peppers for sale in "Little Italy," St. Clair Avenue West.

Above: Shoppers inspect the cheese on offer in a shop in St. Lawrence Market.

Left: For many people, a visit to St. Lawrence Market early on Saturday morning is part of the weekend routine.

Above: Farmers sell fresh produce in season in St. Lawrence Market.

Right: Fresh fish swimming in ice in Kensington Market.

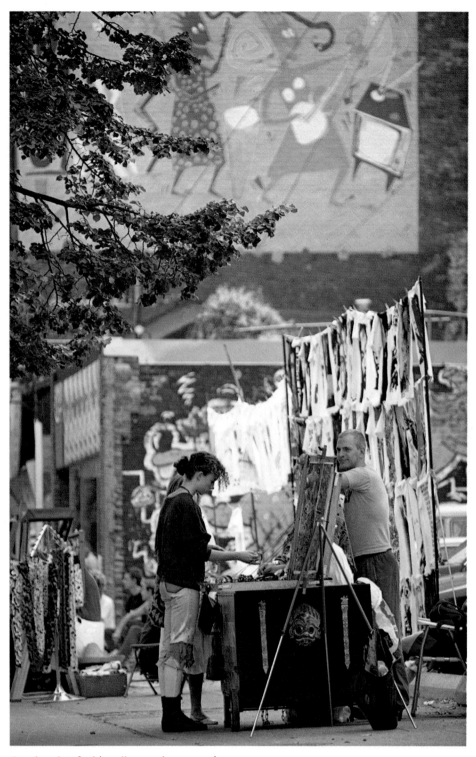

Art, handcrafted jewellery and very modern
fashions are offered for sale by street
vendors on Queen Street West.

A moment for quiet contemplation in Kensington Market.

Keeping the pavement clean in Kensington
Market.

The Peter Pan restaurant was among the
first in a wave of small businesses on Queen
Street West that established the area's
youthful ambience.

Honest Ed's Bargain House is the least
unobtrusive business belonging to one of
the city's most colourful entrepreneurs,
Edwin Mirvish.

Opposite page: The intersection of Yonge and
Dundas is one of the busiest in Toronto.

The Yonge Street "Strip" is always busy,
somewhat tacky, and never dull.

The garment district, on and around
Spadina Avenue, has lots to offer to the
browser and bargain-hunter.

Yorkville, once a haven for hippies, has
become a chic shopping district.

Opposite page: In summer, Yorkville cafes
move out on to the pavement, providing
patrons with an ideal prospect from which
to watch passersby.

Above: A Bloor Street shop window.

Left: Flowers near the intersection of Dundas and Yonge.

A restaurant in Yorkville salutes the Festival
of Festivals.

Excellent new, used and antiquarian bookstores have proliferated on Queen Street West.

A shopper leaves one of the exclusive stores located on Bloor Street.

Toronto in winter.

The Eaton Centre: an indoor avenue
designed to resemble a ship.

Almost anything in the way of fashion, from
furs to frippery, is available in the Garment
District.

Looking north on Yonge Street from Front.
It's about thirty-four miles to the end of
Yonge as originally laid out by the city's
founder, John Graves Simcoe.

The main entrance to the King Edward
Hotel on King Street East.

The King Edward Hotel's main lobby.

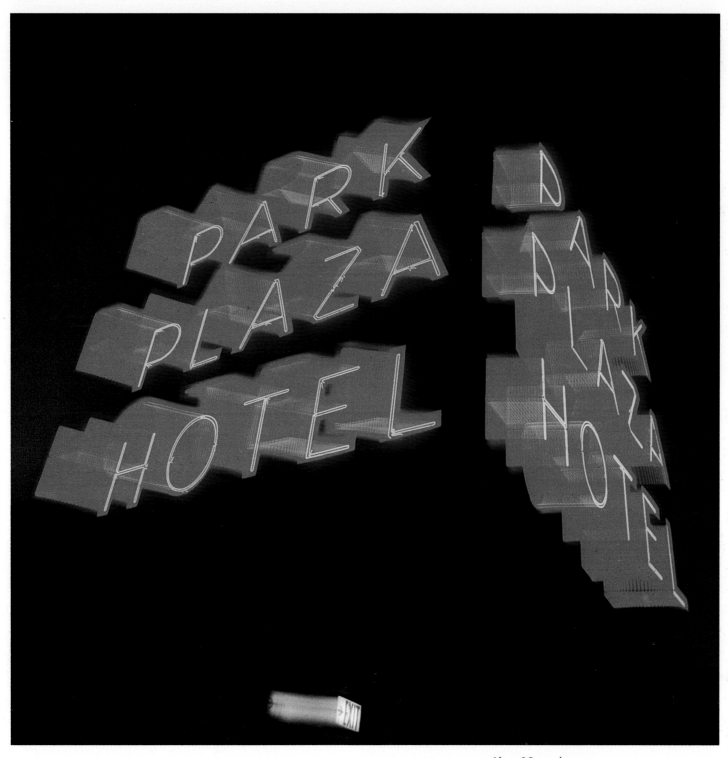

Above: Neon signage.

Opposite page: The view from the rooftop bar
of the Park Plaza Hotel.

The Christmas decorations at Harbourfront
have a nautical twist.

The shopping and condominium complex at Queen's Quay.

The Harbour Castle Westin hotel overlooks
the yachts at play in Lake Ontario.

The Royal York Hotel peers past the shoulders of taller buildings towards the lake.

Photographic Credits